MW00626273

PROTECTING YOUR
RETIREMENT

PROTECTING YOUR RETIREMENT

A Personal Guide
to Understanding and Planning for
a Safe and Secure Retirement

BRAD RHODES

Expert
Press
www.ExpertPress.net

PROTECTING YOUR RETIREMENT:
A Personal Guide to Understanding and Planning for
a Safe and Secure Retirement

Copyright © 2021 Brad Rhodes
All rights reserved.
Printed in the United States of America.

ISBN-13: 978-1-956220-02-5

—Disclaimer—
The information provided in this book is for informational purposes only and is not intended to be a source of advice or credit analysis with respect to the material presented. The information and/or documents contained in this book do not constitute legal or financial advice and should never be used without first consulting with an insurance and/or a financial professional to determine what may be best for your individual needs.

The publisher and the author do not make any guarantee or other promise as to any results that may be obtained from using the content of this book. You should never make any investment decision without first consulting with your own financial advisor and conducting your own research and due diligence. To the maximum extent permitted by law, the publisher and the author disclaim any and all liability in the event any information, commentary, analysis, opinions, advice, and/or recommendations contained in this book prove to be inaccurate, incomplete, or unreliable or result in any investment or other losses.

Although the author and publisher have made every effort to ensure that the information in this book was correct at press time, the author and publisher do not assume and hereby disclaim any liability to any party for any loss, damage, or disruption caused by errors or omissions, whether such errors or omissions result from negligence, accident, or any other cause.

Content contained or made available through this book is not intended to and does not constitute legal advice or investment advice, and no attorney-client relationship is formed. The publisher and the author are providing this book and its contents on an "as is" basis. Your use of the information in this book is at your own risk.

CONTENTS

Introduction: What's Keeping You Up at Night? 1

Chapter 1
Top Priority: Protect Yourself from the Unknowns 7

Chapter 2
Women: More Unknowns Mean More Planning 17

Chapter 3
Pensions: A Thing of the Past 29

Chapter 4
IRAs, 401(k) Plans: Today's "Pension" 39

Chapter 5
The Stock Market: We've Been Blessed 45

Chapter 6
Taxes: What Goes Down Must Come Back Up 51

Chapter 7
Inflation: Another Hidden Tax 57

Chapter 8
The "A" Word: Annuities 63

Chapter 9
Long-Term Care: A Gift for Your Family 71

Chapter 10
The Holy Grail: Guaranteed Income for Life.............. 81

Conclusion
A New ERA: Skipping the Worry of Retirement 87

About the Author 91

Introduction:
What's Keeping You Up at Night?

Over many years in my financial advisory practice, I've accumulated a great deal of experience with Medicare enrollment and retirement planning in general. That experience has made me realize something: Most retirement-aged folks are a lot like my wife and me.

Folks in our stage of life tend to be financially conservative as we approach retirement age—which, of course, is a good thing. It's not that we have a strong aversion to the stock market; it's just that we've come to understand the risks better.

It's also foremost in our minds that when the paychecks stop, we're going to have to rely on our investments to carry us through our golden years of retirement.

It's been some time since I started thinking about how my wife and I would need to plan for our retirements. Naturally, my experience in professional practice made one thing clear: Like my retirement-aged clients, we were going to need a *guaranteed income for life.*

That's what this book is about.

Many of my clients came to me because they were worried about how they'd be able to fund their retirements. It's the kind of thing that keeps folks like us up at night!

If that describes you—now or in the future—this book is for you.

Get Back to Resting Easy at Night

When you have a *guaranteed income for life*—money that's safely invested in places where it can grow but won't be lost in the stock market "casino"—sleep comes much more easily!

I'm not saying you need to get 100 percent of your portfolio out of the stock market. But as you approach or begin retirement, you start to realize that the more of your investment you can safely protect, the better off you'll be in the long run.

Here are some of the things we'll explore in this book, not only to fully illustrate the need for that *guaranteed income for life*, but also to show just how you can create it for yourself and your loved ones:

- How to protect yourself from "the unknowns"
- The reasons women have special retirement planning needs
- How do-it-yourself products, such as individual retirement accounts (IRAs), have replaced traditional pensions
- The impact of taxes and inflation on your retirement (and your health care)
- The truth—good, bad, and ugly—about the "A" word (Annuities)
- Ways to use today's best financial products to truly establish your own *guaranteed income for life*

Why I Wrote This Book

Not long ago, a seventy-year-old client who had lost her husband came to see me. She was very sad, of course. Can you imagine being married fifty years and then losing the love of your life? She was also a bit lost.

Her story is not atypical of those of her generation. Her husband's career had provided virtually all their family's income over many years, and he had been the one who'd made all the decisions about money, insurance, investing, and so forth. Now, he was gone. And this nice lady was at a loss as to what to do next. It's not that she lacked intelligence (far from it), but she just didn't have any experience with the kinds of decisions she now needed to make.

She had "help," of course, from her adult children. But they were not in agreement as to what she should do.

Luckily, one of her kids suggested she visit me and look into how she could use what her husband left her to establish her own *guaranteed income for life*. Her son knew that the money she had from insurance and inheritance was all she could count on to carry her through the rest of her life—and that she clearly couldn't put it at risk.

We thoroughly scanned the market and finally found the client a vehicle that would allow her money to grow at a modest rate, but absolutely would not be at risk of loss.

I can't tell you how grateful she was. And though sound financial planning can't erase the difficult emotions surrounding the death of a dear loved one, it is extremely gratifying to me that a solution like this can at least provide some comfort and relief to clients like this nice lady.

Thanks to countless cases like this one, over the years, I've developed a true *passion* for advising and guiding folks who need help planning for their retirement.

Personal Inspiration

From the beginning of my professional practice in financial advice, I've been extremely blessed to have been "trained" by one of the very best advisors in the entire country.

That "trainer" happened to be my dad. He taught me very early not only to treat people like you'd want to be treated, but to *treat people like you'd want your mother to be treated.*

That statement alone had a big impact on me. It has shaped the way I work with clients, from the beginning of my practice until today.

Take a look at the photo of my dad with my brothers and me. He is now eighty-one years of age, and we still talk business together. He's still helping his clients! He may not work as hard as he used to, but he's still a major blessing to the folks who are lucky enough to benefit from his advice (and, of course, to me).

I feel highly blessed to have the ability to talk over every idea, business and personal, with my dad. He has been a major inspiration for my financial planning practice. My father and the many clients I've been able to help plan their best retirements were my inspiration for writing this book.

I want to pass as much of that blessing as I can on to you!

Introduction

Brad (second from left) with his brothers and father.

Chapter 1

Top Priority:
Protect Yourself from the Unknowns

It's a familiar and fairly common story that has played out many times throughout my career: A couple in their late fifties or early sixties comes to me for advice on planning for retirement. Usually, they realize that there are many things about retirement that they don't know or understand, but feel it's time to get it figured out. They recognize that they don't know what they don't know! It can seem overwhelming.

As a specialist in retirement planning, it's my job to educate my clients on the variables that will end up determining their ability to enjoy the retirement they've been working for, and looking forward to, their whole adult lives.

No one knows the future, not exactly, anyway—not down to the penny. But it's my job to know what my clients don't know and help them plan for those "unknowns" that may well threaten their retirement.

Markets, taxes, rules, regulations—they're all parts of the retirement puzzle that are constantly changing and evolving. Understandably, my clients don't tend to focus on things like the latest IRS rule changes or the interrelationships between societal trends and market growth.

Clients often ask me how I'm able to keep up with all these changes and trends. And I tell them to ask my wife; she'll confirm that I'm not great at fixing things around the house (or under the hood of the car) because I've worked to develop a different collection of skills. The know-how I've developed over the years revolves around helping people retire *well*. That's my passion, and that's where I focus my energy.

So, I can't predict the future for my clients—I don't have a crystal ball—but I can tell them which variables ("unknowns") to watch out for and give them ideas on how to protect themselves and their retirement from those spooky specters.

Some Folks Might Be Resting (Too) Peacefully

Lately, I've discovered an interesting trend: Many members of the currently retiring generation might NOT be all that worried about the unknowns that will inevitably affect their retirement.

Some retiring folks have developed the ability to "live in the moment," which is probably a good thing from a mental-health standpoint. But they're not even thinking about what retirement will look like until, perhaps, their adult children start asking questions about their plans for the future.

Sometimes, those questions begin to awaken the need for a retiring couple to give their retirement planning some thought, even while they're still in the "heat of battle" in their careers and lives.

Another typical scenario is when a couple nearing or at retirement age is suddenly confronted with the need to care for elderly parents. Sometimes, seeing and experiencing elderly parents' needs and wants forces those caring for them to start thinking about their own futures.

I can't tell you how many clients have told me about that "awakening" experience and how surprised they were to gain a new understanding of the needs and challenges of retirement.

Whether earlier or later in "the game," there's generally a point when folks at or near retirement age start to realize there are some unknown variables out there that they need to start planning for.

That's when they might start tossing and turning a bit!

The Obvious, Biggest Worry

Quite appropriately, my retiring clients usually start with the obvious question: Will we have enough money for the retirement we envision?

It seems like a simple question, but even this one has some "hidden" variables most folks haven't anticipated.

- *If I pass away first, will our retirement income be sufficient to take care of my spouse?* Let's take Social Security as an example. Say you're a couple depending on Social Security income in retirement. The husband draws $2,500 per month, and his wife gets $1,400. You might not realize it, but if mister passes away, missus can now take over the higher draw ($2,500), *but she doesn't get both checks.* One of the two checks goes away when a spouse dies.

- *Will my spouse's expenses be cut roughly in half if I die first?* Some couples imagine that "about half" of their retirement income will be sufficient to cover "about half" of the expenses. But it's never correct. Some major expenses will not diminish at all; the surviving spouse is usually left with expenses that aren't much different from those the couple had to pay. A surviving spouse will just have less income with which to pay those expenses—unless they've made a plan that anticipates this scenario.
- *What if I die before I can put a solid plan in place?* That's certainly one of the big worries keeping folks up at night, and it's why more and more clients are starting to plan for retirement much earlier than they might otherwise have done so.
- *Is it possible I could outlive my retirement plan?* Often, folks who have taken on eldercare duties for their loved ones develop this concern. They may even have seen their parents experience this very phenomenon.

What If?

I've met many retirement-aged folks who are susceptible to what I call "what-if retirement."

It's hard for some people to grasp (at least at first), but the distribution (income checks) you draw from your retirement investments needs what I call a Goldilocks's approach: It needs to be *just right.*

Some retirees take too little monthly distribution, often because they can't get past the what-if mentality. What if *this* happens? What if *that* happens? If this what-if approach persists throughout their golden years, these retirees often leave more money behind than they intended and never end up *enjoying* their retirement as they could have.

Then there are the retirees who live a little high on the hog, as the expression goes. These people don't have an appropriate sense of the what-ifs, so they draw too much money every month and deplete their investments quickly. And they're often the ones who suddenly encounter an event they hadn't anticipated and find themselves struggling to make ends meet.

That's why it's important to have a smart plan for retirement—one that keeps the piggy bank safe but also includes some money in reserve to provide flexibility and cover life's what-ifs.

Cash in the Mattress

Some people simply don't trust the products, institutions, or investment vehicles in which their retirement money is invested.

We've all heard about the well-publicized cases of scams and failed institutions that have wiped out many people's retirement savings, money they were counting on to live comfortably in their sunset years.

And then there are worries—often exacerbated by the media—that certain societal trends will likely deplete various pensions and other retirement programs in the not-so-distant future.

These worries certainly have some validity. But taking a cash-in-the-mattress approach isn't the answer. That mattress cash won't continue to grow, and as you deplete it to pay expenses, it will continue to diminish. When it's gone, it's gone! Since you probably won't actually have greenbacks stuffed in a mattress but rather large cash deposits in a bank, your money is still at the mercy of an institution which, itself, is still somewhat at the mercy of those larger external forces that have caused institutions and investments to fail.

We'll cover this in greater detail in the coming pages, but the answer is to have a large part of your portfolio tucked away—not in a mattress but in a vehicle that's fully protected while it continues to grow your nest egg at a modest rate.

The Do-It-Yourself Age

In times past, people got jobs as young adults and often worked their entire careers for a single firm, moving up the company ladder and relying on the company pension they'd receive, along with a gold watch, at retirement time.

Don't look now, but most of those old company pensions are gone, replaced by things like IRAs and 401(k) plans that generally amount to do-it-yourself (DIY) retirement programs.

And it's very challenging to keep up with all the rules associated with these accounts. For instance, the SECURE Act, passed by the federal government in late 2019, changed some of the rules. One example is that you are *required* to start taking distributions from your IRA now at age seventy-two; the required distribution age used to be age seventy and a half. And there are new rules about exhausting your IRA, too. So how do these rules (and their ever-shifting nature) impact your retirement?

Most retirees struggle to keep up with those rules, and rule changes. That's something my clients count on me to do for and with them.

Planning a Healthy Retirement

Health care, in general, has become one of the greatest mysteries in our society, and planning for health care in retirement is one of the very big unknowns these days.

Long-term care (LTC) is a major concern, one many retirees want to plan for to spare their adult offspring a lot of headaches and heartaches (not to mention expenses). Nailing down a good LTC plan is one of the best gifts you can bequeath to the next generation, and we'll cover that in more detail later.

But what about the plain old everyday costs of living as healthy a retirement life as possible?

One very common scenario has to do with prescription drugs and the *donut hole* folks experience as they transition from private insurance to Medicare (one of the specialties of my practice).

For example, there's a common medicine many older folks need these days to maintain a healthy blood flow, and it's very expensive (around $600 per month). Medicare prescription plans offer this drug for an affordable co-pay of around $50. However, at a certain point, people who need this expensive medicine end up exhausting the plan's allowances and finding themselves in the *donut hole*, which means they need to come up with a co-pay *three times more* than they had been paying.

That difference often tips the scale, forcing a retiree to face a difficult choice concerning what to trim from their monthly budget to afford this higher payment for the medicine they need.

You're Going to Need More Money

You will. Thanks to these unknowns, and this is just a partial list.

How will the money you have invested in the stock market be affected by the market's inevitable ups and downs? Can you realize enough market gains to compensate for the risk (when a swift downturn could cost you everything)?

Tax rates are another huge unknown we'll explore in more detail later. It's sufficient to say that with a growing and aging population to take care of and societal changes and world events putting downward pressure on the economy, taxes are not likely to go down during the course of your retirement.

And what about inflation? If you plan your retirement around being able to get goods and services at today's prices, you are probably aware of the fact that you're going to run into trouble.

It all comes down to this: Retirees will need more money in retirement than they may have thought they would. And it's beginning to understand this that brings many of my new clients to my office.

Not Knowing Is Scary

Not knowing what they don't know is scarier for most of my retiring clients than what they find out when they start the planning process and explore these unknowns.

Retirement planning doesn't sound exciting, and maybe that's why some folks put it off. But I can assure you that the exciting things you want to do in your golden years will be much more realistic if you put a plan in place that gives you the *guaranteed income for life* you'll need.

Later, I'll cover in detail my three-step process, the ERA method (the name is a holdover from my days as a college baseball player) that has helped my clients get the retirement they want and need. For now, it's important to understand that retirement planning is more crucial today than ever before.

Timing and Prioritizing

When should you start planning for your retirement and for putting in place that all-important *guaranteed income for life?*

The earlier, the better, of course, but one milepost would be to come to see me *before* you retire and *before* you roll over your employer-sponsored plan.

Perhaps it goes without saying, but things are easier at retirement time when the market is up, especially if it stays up for the first few years of your retirement. It's tougher to handle your planning when the market is down at retirement time.

That's one part of the reason it's smart to get a jump on your retirement planning as early as possible.

But whenever you start planning, there are things you can do—moves you can make at *any* stage—that will really help.

The unknowns are out there (and will always be out there). But planning for them takes away their scariest attributes and gives you the kind of peace of mind everyone is looking for in retirement.

Chapter 2

Women:
More Unknowns Mean More Planning

Not long ago, I was chatting with a retirement-aged couple in my office (which is pretty much what I'm always doing there), and the subject of visiting the dentist came up.

I don't remember exactly why—maybe they had just come from an appointment at the dentist's office. But the gentleman remarked that his wife had "much better teeth" than he had.

"That's because I go to the dentist as a matter of routine," his wife said. "You only go to the dentist when something *hurts*."

We all laughed a little, but it got me thinking: In many ways, that's a great analogy to retirement planning. Smart retirees stay in touch with their financial planning specialists as a matter of course and routinely get advice on the latest opportunities—not just when they're hurting!

Another great analogy comes from tennis. When youngsters start out playing tennis, they just want to get the ball back over the net. They *react*. Pro players, by contrast, *plan their shots* and have studied their opponent's tendencies to come up with their best shot at a plan for victory.

Planning is certainly important for people who want to get their own "best shot" at the retirement they've hoped for. And this is particularly true for women who are members of the currently retiring generation.

Women of this generation typically have more challenges, more unknowns, and more things to think about in their retirement planning than do the men with whom they've shared their lives.

We'll discuss these special challenges in this chapter. But first, I want to relate the stories of a couple of women I've met during the course of my practice to illustrate my point.

A Tale of Two Retired Women

Jim and Jane Johnson (not their real names) came to see me around the time of Jim's retirement to solidify their golden years' plan and explore their options.

The Johnsons liked having invested the bulk of their money in growing equities. Still, after our consultation, they decided to move a relatively small portion of their nest egg into a safe vehicle I suggested. It would allow their money to grow modestly but remain protected from losses in the market.

They particularly liked the idea that if something happened to one of them, the other could move a portion of their savings into this vehicle and create a *guaranteed income for life*.

It was a pretty simple plan. We didn't make a lot of big moves. We just took a portion of their money out of the "casino" and protected it where it could grow at a competitive rate. And that's where the money sat, continuing to grow for about eleven years—at which point Jim passed away.

18

CHAPTER 2: WOMEN

Jane met with me again, and after exploring some options, she decided to go ahead and move that saved money into the guaranteed instrument we had planned for the surviving spouse.

Things worked out well for Jane. She had a guaranteed income coming in; the new income stream nearly made up for the loss of income resulting from the end of Jim's Social Security payments.

Of course, nothing can compensate for the loss of a dear loved one, and Jane still misses Jim terribly. But she doesn't miss his income because we were able to replace nearly all of it. So having enough money to cover her expenses is something Jane doesn't have to worry about, and as a result, she's enjoying a much lower level of stress than she otherwise would.

By the way, I'm a strong believer in the notion that anything you can do to reduce an elderly person's stress—say, a widow like Jane—helps them live longer and happier lives. It's a big part of why I do what I do.

Now, I'm not trying to suggest that your retirement is doomed without my advice, but things turned out much differently for the Grays than they did for the Johnsons.

I met with Grant and Greta Gray (also not their real names) at about the same time in their lives—right around retirement. Naturally, we talked about how to prepare for what things would look like fifteen to twenty years down the road and how to anticipate the many unknowns. Like the Johnsons, the Grays had their nest egg invested largely in the market. Unlike Jim and Jane, the Grays decided to leave things as they were instead of trying to protect a portion of what they had saved.

Since they did engage my services for their Medicare supplemental plans, I was able to stay in touch with Grant and Greta over the years.

About eight years after our first meeting, Grant passed away. It was sudden and unexpected. And five years after his death, for reasons I don't know and about which I won't presume to pass judgment, Greta had spent the lion's share of their savings.

Part of the money had been invested in a low-yield certificate of deposit (CD) and savings accounts, but the majority of the funds were in an IRA.

Now, an IRA is a beautiful instrument with the capacity to provide a lifetime of income if properly set up and used. It's based on the concept of letting your money grow *before* it's taxed and paying the taxes later (when you take withdrawals). By that time, you have captured a lot more growth than you otherwise would have, and you can better afford the tax.

But you can probably guess what I'm about to relate: Greta Gray had been draining her IRA with frequent withdrawals, and with each withdrawal came an added *tax liability*.

That depletion is bad enough. But Greta was also directing the account's custodian to pay the taxes out of the same account, sending checks to the IRS and state while also sending checks to her.

Talk about a double whammy!

I don't know everything about what went on in Greta's life during those years, and again, I don't mean to judge. I know it's hard to focus on making the smartest business decisions when you're grieving and emotionally reeling. But that's why I wish the Grays had decided to move some of their money out of harm's way when I'd first met with them years earlier. If they had, Greta would have some guaranteed income coming to her every month (aside from her Social Security, which is now all she really has).

Not all of us need that forced discipline. In fact, few of us think we need it at retirement time. That's why it's a great idea to plan ahead for a time when, solid as we seem today, we might need that structure in the future.

I'm still in touch with Greta. She still has her Medicare supplement plan with me. But I feel sad about her situation. She's only seventy-seven years young, in great health, and has the kind of good genes that give her every chance of living well into her nineties.

Though she has a lot to be thankful for, she no longer has her savings.

Having treated her IRA like a cash-filled mattress, Greta now faces a harsh reality: *When it's gone, it's gone.*

Women Have More Challenges in Retirement

Though they ended up in very different places financially, Greta and Jane shared a common starting point: Their husbands had been the family's primary breadwinners, as was the case with many married couples of their generation. When the guys passed away, the ladies were left in unfamiliar territory. And that brings us to the specific challenges women face in the generation that's currently somewhere around the retirement stage of their lives.

Let's start by reviewing some of the factors that make retiring today different from what it was just a few years ago—for people of *both* genders.

In his scholarly work, Professor David F. Babbel refers to the coming "financial storm" and five forces that are converging on us today:[1]

- *The demise of pensions.* Retirement used to be "set it and forget it." Now, retirement-aged people have to make all the right moves *themselves* to protect their future.
- *Decreasing returns.* The old pensions from a generation ago enjoyed better returns than the contributions people make to their DIY retirement plans today.
- *More retirees.* The baby boomers—people born right after the troops returned home after World War II—are now retiring, which means a new and greater pressure on our Social Security system.
- *Longer lives (especially for women).* Life expectancy in the United States is significantly greater than in the old days.
- *New demands on younger generations to fund retirees.* Women's retirement needs are particularly challenging to fund.

Already, in the case of the last couple of forces, Dr. Babbel addresses the needs of retiring women as distinctively challenging compared to those of retirement-aged men.

Here are some other factors creating pressure for the baby boomer women in the currently retiring generation:

---

[1] Babbel, David F. "Lifetime Income for Women: A Financial Economist's Perspective." Wharton Financial Institutions Center and New York Life Insurance Company, August 12, 2008. https://ahe.illinois. edu/files/2019/11/Lifetime-Income-for-Women.pdf.

- *Women have been caretakers.* There's an old expression some retirement-aged husbands have used: "When I'm sick, I'm helpless. When my wife is sick, guess what: I'm also helpless." That's because many women of the currently retiring generation —perhaps a majority—have prioritized caretaking (of their children, their parents, and even their spouses) above making or even thinking about money. Women are generally as smart as the husbands who predecease them (often smarter!), but when it comes to financial decisions, a large number of the women in this retiring generation haven't had much practice. Others had marriages where both spouses took active roles in planning for the future; those women generally have more favorable retirement situations simply because they've been in the game for years before their husbands passed away.
- *Women have accumulated less savings.* Related to the primary roles they assumed as caretakers, many women of this generation devoted fewer years of their lives to working outside the home. In fact, women who are retiring now have typically been out of the workforce for *eleven more years* than their husbands. These widows simply weren't able to earn (or save) as much as the men did, for the simple reason that they didn't work as many years. Add to that the glass ceiling, which has kept salaries lower for women of that generation, and it's not hard to understand the reasons for this savings gap.
- *Poor planning has left too many women in a bad spot.* And this poor planning is often a team effort

resulting from their husbands' shortsightedness (not to generalize too much!).

To illustrate this last point, take the typical example of a couple in which the husband worked a long and lucrative career, giving the family the ability to live a good lifestyle. He earned the money and, therefore, assumed the role of chief financial officer for the family and made all the investment decisions.

However, earning money didn't prepare the husband to understand how best to invest it, and he ended up losing a lot of the couple's nest egg in a large, bad investment.

Now he's in his seventies, can't retire, and works himself long and hard to try to recover what he lost. That hard work led to the predictable heart attack, and now his wife is left all by herself to try to figure out what to do next!

It's the typical case of a middle-aged or elderly woman suddenly being thrust into a position of having to make decisions she's had no practice in thinking about.

In an attempt to compensate for their lost savings (and make matters worse), the couple took out a *reverse mortgage*, an instrument that pays a monthly income by slowly depleting the equity on their home. So the wife is now *stuck* in the high-life home, with all its maintenance and upkeep.

The one bright spot in this particular tale is that the husband had the foresight to take out a life insurance policy. For people like this who have failed rather spectacularly in their DIY investment adventures, this is NOT the norm. People like the husband in our story don't generally regard life insurance as income protection for their surviving spouse—but it can be a lifesaver.

The wife put the insurance proceeds in a safe annuity, which is a good move. She has lived well throughout her many years and wants to have cash for herself, but she also wants to leave money to the kids. Unfortunately, in her situation, she can't really have both. Every cash payment reduces her principal, leaving her with less (much less over time) for herself and her children.

This tale is typical of a generation that wants to have it all. For those of you who recall the Helen Reddy song "I Am Woman" from the 1970s, you know that women of that generation (often dubbed the "Me Generation") did want to have it all—career, children, a good lifestyle, everything.

In retirement, women of that generation should be aware that they can, in fact, have it all (or at least get close).

But it takes a lot of smart financial planning to get the have-it-all retirement!

"The Mother-In-Law Plan"

It's the plan my mother-in-law and I came up with to guarantee her the kind of retirement she wanted and deserved. But it's an example of a strong retirement plan for *anyone.*

It's really just a plan for a *guaranteed income for life,* and the cornerstone concept is making sure at least some of your retirement nest egg is out of harm's way, meaning it can't be lost in the Wall Street casino.

My mother-in-law is a very sharp woman. As an architect, she made a good living during her career, and she invested "pretty aggressively" (as she describes it) in her firm's 401(k) retirement plan near the end of her career in the 1980s.

That was a good time for a program like a 401(k). The market was booming, and my mother-in-law's money grew nicely—and quickly. When she retired, her money was in two different accounts, most invested in the stock market.

As my mother-in-law relates it, she would get up every day and immediately jump on her computer to check the market, closely following the ups and downs of her investments. After a few years, she realized two things: First, she grew a little tired of having to babysit her nest egg so closely. Second, she began to realize that since her retirement funds were heavily leveraged in the stock market, she really could end up taking a significant loss at some point.

She set a meeting with her retirement advisor son-in-law (that would be me)—I told you she was sharp!—and started exploring how she could move at least a substantial portion of her portfolio out of harm's way and create a future income she could rely on.

We ended up moving about half of her money into a cutting-edge product known as a fixed index annuity (FIA). In her case, we added a lifetime income benefit as a rider to the investment.

For the first few years after this conversion, the FIA allowed her to participate in market growth without taking on market risk. So, she still got modest growth but had no chance of losing that money since it was invested with a quality company, and the instrument was set up to prevent any losses.

Then, when my mother-in-law turned seventy and a half, she was required by IRS regulation to start taking a *required minimum distribution* from her account. But here's the beautiful part of the FIA: Even though she was now taking disbursements from the account, it was still *growing* at a rate greater than the rate of depletion!

Eventually, she decided to activate the lifetime income benefit, and her income was much higher than her required minimum distribution. Even so, because she had the foresight to set things up the way she did, the income is *guaranteed* for her life, no matter how long she lives.

What makes the Mother-In-Law Plan so attractive is that we were able to get a portion of her money out of harm's way—where she can't lose it—and it continued to grow, even after she started taking distributions from it.

And when she truly reaches that point where she simply does NOT want to keep checking her computer first thing every morning, she doesn't have to. The whole thing is like a speeding aircraft on autopilot.

Money is one thing she doesn't have to worry about for the rest of her life.

Chapter 3

Pensions: A Thing of the Past

If you were a member of the American workforce a generation or so ago, you didn't really need too much in the way of financial planning for retirement.

Your *pension* was set up and managed by your employer, so your retirement was more or less automatic.

You worked fifty or so years for one company, and when your sixty-fifth birthday rolled around, they threw you a nice retirement party and gave you a gold watch. Then, the distributions (monthly paychecks) from your pension started arriving in your mailbox.

It was a worry-free retirement! And those pension payments generally lasted for the rest of your life.

Those days are long gone, though. Other than folks who've retired from government service, you'd be hard-pressed to find someone recently or soon to be retired with a company pension. Certainly, you'd have trouble finding a private-sector pension that's likely to last a retiree and their spouse the rest of their lives.

What Happened to the Traditional Pension?

The demise of the old pension plan resulted from technical reasons related to the market, societal trends, and high finance. I won't go into all the details here, but the following are some commonsense reasons you can't find a pensioner these days.

First, people started living longer. Much longer. These days, general life expectancy is much greater than in the glory days of the pension plans enjoyed by baby boomers and their parents and grandparents. When people began enjoying longer retirements, that meant they were drawing more money from their company pensions, which put tremendous pressure on those funds.

Changes in employee loyalty also caused pressure on pensions. A couple of generations ago, it was quite common for a person to work their entire career for a single pension-providing company. Do you know anyone like that today? Since pension payments to retirees depended on contributions from younger employees, and those younger employees weren't sticking around for their entire careers, the pension concept began to experience some significant wobbles. The cost a company incurred to hire and train people more often meant less money in the till from which to pay retirees.

Then came some well-publicized scandals involving the misuse and nearly outright theft of pension funds. Some of these scandals resulted from company executives realizing they simply couldn't produce the profits their shareholders demanded without "borrowing" from the company pension fund. Other scandals were probably born of more nefarious motivations. In any case, some large pension funds evaporated, leaving their retirees in a very bad spot.

By the way, those big pension plans were often interrelated: When the husband's pension from the steel mill vanished, it put pressure on the wife's pension from the school district, to illustrate one example.

Why didn't companies simply stop worrying about employee retirement altogether? The reason might be found in the phrase "war for talent." If you were a skilled worker who had the choice between Company A and Company B (and Company A offered a retirement plan that Company B didn't), all other things being equal, Company A would likely be your choice.

Put it all together, and it became clear a few years ago that responsible corporate financial executives needed to come up with a different way to offer retirement plans to their employees.

The pension concept fell by the wayside, replaced by the new 401(k) plan.

The 401(k): A "New Economy" Approach

The 401(k) program was a wonderful solution to the changes that led to the pension's demise. It stabilized things for employers and eliminated many of the problems corporations faced when trying to keep retirees paid while receiving less and less from younger employees.

The good traditional pension was a *defined benefit* program, meaning the monthly payout a retiree would receive was set and unchanging (defined). So no matter how much money the fund took in, the pensioner got a defined amount of money each month and could rely on that check, rain or shine. The *variables* were controlled and managed by the company and its financial officers.

For the reasons described earlier, a defined benefit plan would no longer work in a new economy where people changed jobs (sometimes frequently) and lived longer after retirement. The old pension funds simply couldn't keep up the benefit payments, given their steadily dwindling resources.

What was needed was a *defined contribution* system— one in which the employee established their own benefit by making contributions to their individual retirement plan, and the employer simply matched those contributions at a preestablished rate.

Now, the employer could count on (and plan for) the (defined) amount it would need to come up with to match its employees' contributions to their various 401(k) programs. To a large extent, the *variables* now had to be managed by the individual employee.

The IRS also encouraged individuals to invest in *individual retirement accounts* to supplement their 401(k) benefits. As described earlier, the IRA is an account that grows on a *tax-deferred* basis, meaning the funds aren't taxed until they're withdrawn and can thereby grow at a faster rate while they remain in the account.

Just about all of these accounts—both 401(k) and IRA—are linked in some way to the stock market. Employers and financial institutions don't just keep cash in a vault from which to pay your retirement checks. Instead, they invest that money, largely in the stock market.

As we'll explore later, the stock market has been a great place to invest for some time now. We've been blessed. But only a fool would think their money is safe and their proceeds guaranteed when that money is significantly leveraged in the market.

The Pluses (and Minuses)

As described, the 401(k) and IRA were great innovations that solved a lot of problems for both companies and their retirees. However, as is the case with most things these days, when you retire and roll your 401(k) over to an IRA, this presents both benefits and challenges to the modern retiree.

You could think of the IRA as DIY retirement since, to a large extent, you as an individual now have responsibility for managing the variables that determine your gains (or losses).

But that's a double-edged sword that includes both pluses and minuses for the retiring person or couple:

- *More choices (and more possibilities to analyze).* You can choose the level to which you contribute to your company's 401(k) plan. For most plans, you can even pick which funds or types of funds (collections of stocks, bonds, and other instruments) your money is invested in. With an IRA, you get to choose the institution in which your nest egg is invested, which means you can shop around for the custodian that you think will do the best job of investing (and growing) your money. Of course, that means you have to spend much more time and energy than your granddad did getting smart about the stock market, the economy, and various financial institutions.

- *More growth potential (and MUCH more risk).* As mentioned, these funds are almost always leveraged to some extent in the stock market. Even the bond market carries some risk. While things are great, and growth is accelerated when the markets are up—what goes up generally does come down! You could sustain a serious loss to your retirement fund when it's leveraged in these markets. So while you get to make choices that might increase the growth of your portfolio, those choices always come with greater risk.
- *More portability (less stability).* You can take your 401(k) plan with you and *roll it* into your new employer's program when you change jobs. When you retire or change jobs, you can also *roll it over* into an IRA. So you aren't bound to one employer for the duration of your career. However, every time you make a change, you have to learn a new program, analyze a new set of choices, and wonder whether the growth of your fund will increase or decrease as a result of the change in management. And, again, your money is still at least partially at risk in the stock market "casino." In many cases, it's completely at risk.

These aren't the only considerations. As the chief custodian of your DIY retirement plan, you not only have to figure out how and when to roll things over into new accounts, you also have to determine when to start drawing distributions from those accounts (and how much to pay yourself). You're on your own with the *what-if* retirement questions we discussed in Chapter 1. And what about managing your tax liabilities in the smartest way?

Granddad had a LOT less to worry about as he approached retirement!

An Account Is Not a "Plan"

Ask most folks approaching retirement whether they have a retirement plan and, if they say they do, they're likely considering their 401(k) or IRA (or both) to be that plan.

But those aren't plans. They're accounts. A true plan is what you would create (often in consultation with a financial planning pro) as a roadmap for how to best *use those accounts.*

For instance, you might want to take a big chunk of money out of your retirement fund for something fun, such as a once-in-a-lifetime vacation or a cool purchase like a boat or a second home. To some extent, that's exactly what you saved that money for and waited all those years to do!

And if you have a true *plan* for your retirement, you'd understand how to make that fun expenditure without losing too much of your nest egg.

That's because a real retirement plan is not a guessing game. But, unfortunately, too many retirees guess that they can make a big, fun expenditure based on what they think the markets will do or how healthy and robust their bodies will be in the future—and too many of those guesses turn out to be wrong.

Some folks feel pretty good about how they're positioned for retirement, having rolled over a nice 401(k) plan and/or saved a decent amount in an IRA. But for the smartest of these folks, eventually, a subtle shift occurs in their thinking—they begin to realize they need to eliminate at least some of the guesswork. They need a true plan for the distribution of their retirement funds.

And they need to get at least some of their nest egg out of the stock market casino and harm's way and into instruments that can offer them a *guaranteed income for life*.

In the next chapter, we'll start taking a look at some of today's top tools for executing just such a smart decision.

Forced Discipline

Not long ago, I received a notice that a rather youngish retired client had taken another draw from her retirement, basically draining her account.

Of course, I advised caution. It takes *discipline* to manage your DIY retirement these days.

As I explained to her, the good traditional pension was automatic; it required no management or choices on the retiree's part and did not allow a retiree to take more or less than their defined benefit each month.

The old pension was a form of forced discipline. The bad news was that you didn't have any choices to make. The good news was that you didn't have any choices to make!

With the products that have replaced the old pension, such as 401(k) and IRA accounts, a retiree basically has bulk money sitting in an account, and they need to exercise great discipline not to touch it when they can't afford the loss.

What will happen to the client who drains her retirement account when she *runs out of money?*

Remember the Tale of Two Retired Women from an earlier chapter? Greta did just what my recent client did, leaving nothing but her Social Security. Unfortunately, the kind of retirement she hoped for was gone.

There are products you can take advantage of today that can restore a little of that forced discipline—in that a monthly distribution amount is set, and you have that income *guaranteed for life.*

That's the sort of thing that brings retirees reduced stress, easier sleep, and a solution to the *what-if* questions so many people struggle with.

And it's within your reach!

Chapter 4

IRAs, 401(k) Plans: Today's "Pension"

As mentioned, defined contribution accounts, such as the 401(k) and IRA, are the financial tools that have replaced Granddad's old defined benefit pension.

They aren't retirement plans. A retirement plan is what you and I map out as the best way to use these accounts. So, the 401(k) and the IRA are valuable tools in designing a true retirement plan, and they can be key essential building blocks to creating your *guaranteed income for life*.

Gamblers and Savers

Financial planners work with a variety of investors, and our clients usually run along a continuum from least to most risk averse—from the most aggressive gambler mentality investors to the most conservative saver types.

Aggressive investors are looking to maximize portfolio growth and are less concerned with the amount of risk they have to take on to get that growth. In contrast, savers are less concerned with growth than with minimizing risk.

That gambler mindset might work well when the stock market is roaring, and the investor is still employed in their career—when they're in the *accumulation* phase of their financial lives. They're still earning money and trying to build as hefty a nest egg as they can.

It's easy to find financial planners who specialize in working with aggressive investors in this accumulation phase.

My practice is different. I specialize in helping people develop solid plans for *distribution* of the nest egg they've accumulated, a critically important (and sometimes overlooked) part of the retirement planning process.

You have to be more careful with your money once the paychecks stop and you have to rely only on savings. And making a plan for exactly how you're going to *pay yourself* from your accumulated nest egg is the heart and soul of true retirement planning.

Done wrong, distribution from a 401(k) or IRA can lead to real disaster in your golden years. But a well-executed distribution plan can be worth its weight in gold!

I work primarily with conservative savers, helping them create smart plans for paying themselves through retirement. From the standpoint of taxes and the other unknowns that we've discussed, having a solid distribution plan is at least as important as having a plan for growth and accumulation.

It may not be the sexy part of retirement planning. But great distribution planning can make all the difference between disappointment and peace of mind in retirement.

Optimizing the Way You Pay Yourself

It gives me great satisfaction to work with pre-retirees who want to make the most of their 401(k) savings and retirees who understand their IRAs are income tools to use in paying themselves now that their careers are no longer generating paychecks.

While the accumulation phase is the time to take calculated risks and go for portfolio growth, the distribution phase is all about protecting and conserving what you've accumulated, getting the distributions you pay yourself *just right* (as Goldilocks would say).

After all, what good is even a 10 percent growth in your portfolio if that extra money is going to be wiped out by whatever plans the IRS is making for your money?

As mentioned, the IRS requires that you begin taking distributions from your IRA at a certain point; thanks to the recent SECURE Act, that point is now age seventy-two. (Until 2020, the required age to begin IRA distribution was age seventy and a half.)

So, the goal is to take into account taxes, inflation, and all the other unknowns to optimize your *distributions* (the amounts you pay yourself on a regular basis).

That's where the advice of a financial planning professional who specializes in distribution is extremely valuable—even crucial.

Often, a retiring person or couple only needs to make small moves in their portfolio at retirement time to create a safe, sensible distribution plan. Others need a more comprehensive "road map."

And retirement planning is not just for the wealthy! In fact, the less you've been able to accumulate, the more important it is to protect yourself against losses.

Folks who fail to secure their retirement are often the ones who haven't taken advantage of what a professional retirement planner can offer.

Is Your Nest Egg Truly Safe?

Sometimes I run across retirement-aged folks who tell me they're conservative investors. For example, when I ask them whether an $80,000 loss from their $300,000 portfolio would upset them, the typical response is that such a loss would be "a disaster." Yet when we examine their portfolio, they're surprised to learn that such a loss could be a real possibility.

Often, retiring investors have their money invested in instruments that aren't nearly as safe as they think. And absent the advice of a professional planner, they would never have come to that realization.

Your IRA nest egg might be invested, essentially, in the stock market. And when the market experiences a "correction" or significant loss, it can be difficult (often impossible) for your retirement savings to recover and reach previous levels as you wait for the market to recover.

On the other hand, what about the ultraconservative saver whose nest egg is sitting in a bank savings account? That retiree will find it nearly impossible to enjoy any growth in their portfolio because they're constantly forced to deplete the principal in order to cover expenses.

That's why it's so important to move your nest egg into instruments that permit you to optimize your distribution to make sure the way you're paying yourself is *just right*.

Remember the "Mother-In-Law Plan?" After $60,000 in distribution, this wise lady still had the same principal she started with! And that principal was continuing to grow.

A Solid Plan That Goes with the Flow

When you have *guaranteed income for life,* your nest egg is truly safe. But if you're taking advantage of the advice of a distribution-focused planning professional, and you're using the best of today's retirement tools, your plan can also provide the flexibility you'd need if life throws you a curveball.

A few years ago, I met the Jensens, a couple who were getting ready to retire. They owned a small business and wanted to pass it on to their son.

Mr. and Mrs. Jensen had each been contributing to a traditional IRA plan, and together they had accumulated an impressive nest egg.

Now that they were going to retire and stop bringing in "new money" paychecks, their goal was to set up their IRAs to generate enough income to properly supplement their Social Security.

Both told me, "We are not gamblers. We need something that guarantees that we won't lose any of our money."

Naturally, these are precisely the type of conservative investors with whom I like to work. (When I meet with a gambler type, I usually can tell right away that our philosophies aren't going to mesh!)

We found the Jensens a "just-right" instrument to provide them with the *guaranteed income for life* they wanted.

Mr. and Mrs. Jensen were planning to start paying themselves from their nest egg right away. But things change, don't they?

As they were poised to hand the business off to their son, he realized that he needed trustworthy and knowledgeable employees. Who better than Mom and Dad? So he asked them to continue working in the business.

"New money" paychecks were back—and the Jensens decided they didn't need to tap their IRA accounts right away.

Those accounts stayed safe and continued to "cook," as I describe it. And the longer you're able to leave your nest egg IRA account alone and let it "cook"—continue to grow and accumulate interest—the bigger your distributions will be once you begin taking them.

The Jensens were smart with their retirement planning, of course. They knew the gambler mentality would not serve them well as they approached retirement.

Gambler investors tend to love the stock market. Again, they want growth and don't care as much about risk.

So let's take a look at the stock market and its impact on retirement planning.

Chapter 5

The Stock Market:
We've Been Blessed

With the advent of the 401(k) in the early 1980s, average Americans were introduced to the stock market in far greater numbers than ever before.

Their retirement nest eggs were no longer *set it and forget it*, as they were in the days of their dad's or granddad's pensions. Since these "new" 401(k) accounts were generally anchored in the stock market, folks had to pay a lot more attention to what was happening in the market in order to be smart about which funds (or groups of funds) to use.

And when it came time to retire, folks with 401(k) accounts faced a challenge their parents hadn't had to deal with, which was what to do with the nest egg now that the "new money" paychecks were no longer coming in?

In general, eggs are fragile, right? You have to handle them carefully, or you end up with a cracked mess on your hands!

So referring to your retirement savings as a nest egg is fully appropriate! You have to handle it with great care. And while your parents and grandparents had their pensions handled for them, the 401(k) ushered in a new era in which retirees have to handle their nest eggs themselves.

The wise retiree gets help from a financial advisor who knows how to handle nest eggs with the care they need and make sure clients are set up with a safe, secure, *guaranteed income for life.*

Caring for the Lump-Sum Nest Egg

As we discussed, in the old days of the employee pension, the employee contributed to a *defined benefit* plan which provided a fixed-amount (defined benefit) retirement check the retiree would receive every month.

The 401(k) changed that. (There are still a few defined benefit plans out there, mostly in the government sector.) As a *defined contribution* account, the 401(k) provides employees with a range of fixed amounts they can *contribute* to their nest egg. The account grows (or doesn't!) according to the performance of the equities (stocks, bonds, etc.) that the account is invested in.

Then, at retirement time, the employee receives a *lump sum*—the entirety of their nest egg—and has to figure out what to do with it.

No longer can a retiree count on a fixed monthly check—*unless* they've made a plan for the *distribution* of those funds that would come close to replicating the old pension payments.

Those 401(k) funds have been growing on a tax-deferred basis, which means the taxes aren't paid until the funds are distributed. So, the retiree might have the option of simply liquidating their 401(k) account upon retirement, but they would take a significant hit from the taxman. For that reason, most people try to come up with a wiser plan for distribution.

This lump-sum retirement created both a blessing and a curse. It's a blessing in that you have a significant amount of money (in most cases) to reinvest by rolling the lump sum, all or part, into something like an IRA. But the curse is that the retiree now has to figure out how to make that lump sum last for the rest of their life (and their spouse's life), taking into account tax rates, inflation, longer life expectancies, and the other unknowns we discussed in Chapter 1.

Meanwhile, many of the retiree's choices in terms of what to do with their lump sum nest egg still leave their retirement money at the mercy of an ever-volatile stock market!

The 401(k) is a blessing—but it brings with it side effects that can create significant worry and anxiety the parents of today's retiree never had to face. And anxiety is one of the worst things a retirement-aged person can have to deal with. It certainly doesn't give them the best chance to live a longer, happier life.

That's why it's an extremely smart move to seek advice and help from a financial pro who's been down this road with many other clients and who knows how to protect that fragile nest egg. Such an advisor will certainly suggest moving at least a substantial portion of a client's retirement savings out of harm's way and out of the Wall Street casino.

It's the only way to provide a retiree and their spouse with a *guaranteed income for life.*

We've Been Blessed

It's a fact that most financial planners are more adept and experienced at planning for *accumulation* than for *distribution.*

Many retirees place their money with accumulation-oriented planners, and things can work out okay for them when the market is up and moving higher.

In the United States, we've been blessed by a pretty strong stock market for a number of years. That's probably why many financial advisors focus on accumulation—racking up nice numbers for their clients—and may have taken their eye off the ball in terms of distribution.

But the stock market is subject to the age-old rule: What goes up must (eventually) come down. So when your nest egg is invested primarily or exclusively in the market, you might not realize it, but your money is at risk. You could lose every penny.

That's because while we've truly been blessed by an ever-growing market in recent years, that growth is considered by many smart analysts to have been at least partially *artificial.*

The government can pull certain levers that help prop up (or even pump up) the stock market. Anyone who's been following financial and governmental matters knows that this artificial support for the market simply can't go on forever. We've seen the political winds change drastically in just the past handful of years. With those changes, we invariably get changes in the philosophy that drives the federal government's involvement with the economy—and the stock market.

These days, even the average news consumer is aware of things like the national debt, deficit spending, massive entitlement programs, and other factors that are sure to affect changes in the stock market.

That's a big reason more and more retirees see the advantage of working with a financial advisor specializing in distribution, "safe money," and that all-important *guaranteed income for life.*

* * *

You wouldn't have trouble finding a top-notch financial advisor to help with the accumulation phase of your retirement planning.

But very few know the ins and outs of the IRA distribution laws.

To some extent, I've invested in the stock market myself; I'm certainly not against it. I'm just also a big believer in having some of your nest egg in a safe place, so it will be there when it comes time to start paying yourself.

True distribution planning is such an integral part of retiring with a safe, guaranteed lifetime income. That's why I specialize in precisely that area of retirement planning, and why I find such great passion in helping folks plan how they'll pay themselves throughout retirement.

The goal is to make sure your retirement dollars last as long as you do!

Chapter 6

Taxes: What Goes Down
Must Come Back Up

Many people today may not even realize that there was a time when there was no income tax at all in this country. However, while those days are long gone (for more than a century now), historically speaking, we're in a period of relatively low taxation in the United States.

The top-bracket tax rate as of this writing is around 39 percent. Not long ago, that top rate was around 70 percent.

As the political winds blow and things change, different philosophies of government and economics gain prominence at different times. When things change politically, so does the rate of tax Americans are required to pay.

Politics and societal shifts aside, the point is that things are always changing. Unfortunately, we've arrived at a point in American history where the coming changes are almost certainly not going to be in your favor as a retiree.

Just as we've been in an extended period of stock market growth, our taxes have been low for a while now. The market is governed to some extent by the old saying: *What goes up must come down.* However, you could consider the federal income tax rate oppositely: *What goes down must eventually come back UP.*

This means you're almost certainly going to be liable for more tax in the not-too-distant future.

And, as I've pointed out, that means we're all going to need more money in retirement than many of us have thought we would.

Funding Entitlements

Developed nations these days offer *entitlement programs* to their citizens. Some examples in the United States include Social Security, Medicaid and Medicare, food stamps, and other welfare programs.

In some countries, the government also pays for LTC for its citizens. However, the tax rates in those countries are astronomical compared with ours.

These entitlement programs have always been hot-button topics for politicians, and they certainly have a large and growing importance in our political and social discourse today.

Sometimes candidates offer new or growing entitlement programs on the campaign trail. At times, they're "demanded" by various interest groups in the population. And sometimes, it's hard to tell which came first, just like the chicken and the egg. But eventually, entitlement program growth becomes virtually expected. The money the government must put into these programs is vast and continues to grow.

Whether pushed by elected officials or demanded by public interest groups, entitlement programs are here to stay, and their growth appears to have no end in sight.

How does the government fund these programs?

The answer is obvious: These programs are often referred to as *redistribution or transfer payments*. The money comes from some citizens in the form of higher and higher taxes, and it's transferred or redistributed to other citizens in the form of entitlement benefit payments.

That's one reason you can count on your taxes going up in the near and distant future and why you're going to need more money than you may have planned for in retirement.

Cracking into Your Nest Egg

Whether in a 401(k) account or IRA, your money's been growing on a *tax-deferred basis* (taxes have not been paid on that money). As a result, you've gained interest in a higher principal than you otherwise would have.

You can imagine the federal government, with all these huge and growing entitlement payments to cover, is eager to crack into your nest egg and start taxing it!

That's why taxes can creep into your retirement funds, sometimes to an even greater extent than they creep into your income during your working years.

I talk a lot about IRAs because there are so many subtleties most folks don't know about them. There's also a LOT to be gained from the powerful income tool that is your IRA if you are able to take advantage of some basic principles and explore the options an IRA offers.

Thanks to the SECURE Act of 2019 that I mentioned earlier, you are now required to begin taking distributions from your IRA at age seventy-two. But how much are you required to take, and what exactly will that mean to your nest egg as you move forward in retirement?

The IRS uses a calculation chart to determine your mandatory distributions, but the numbers on that chart change with some regularity. Let's take a look at one example from a recent version of this calculation.

At age seventy-two, the IRS expects you to draw money from your IRA in the first year as though you will be drawing distributions for 25.6 years. Of course, it doesn't mean your actual life expectancy is 97.6 years (though you certainly might live to that age); they are just arbitrary figures used to calculate what the IRS expects you to withdraw from your IRA.

So, assume your nest egg is around $300,000. If you do the math, you're supposed to withdraw about 1/25 of the total in that first year, which amounts to about $12,000. And the IRS now gets to tax that money.

As tax rates increase, it would not be surprising to see that the "tax hit" your money takes each year could reach 50 percent. So, that $12,000 could quickly become $6,000.

What's more, based on the IRS's calculation chart, the *percentage* of your IRA you're required to withdraw *increases* each year. Once the IRS has cracked into your nest egg, they want to tax you more each year!

A "Hidden" Tax

The obvious taxes are bad enough. But, unfortunately, there's more to consider. Retirees face many "hidden taxes."

For instance, did you know your Social Security benefits could also be taxed at the ordinary (and ever-growing) rate you'd pay on your income?

Depending on your *combined income* (also known as *provisional income*), the taxman could take a bite out of up to 85 percent of your Social Security check. This provisional income number is determined by adding your adjusted gross income (AGI), non-taxable interest (such as interest on municipal bonds), and half of your Social Security benefit.

For example, in 2019, single tax filers with a combined income of $25,000 to $34,000 paid taxes on 50 percent of their Social Security benefits (married couples filing jointly paid this tax if their combined income was $32,000 to $44,000). And if the taxpayers' combined income was higher than these ranges, they paid taxes on 85 percent of their Social Security check.

What happens if: 1) you and your spouse get Social Security checks totaling, say, $5,000 per month, 2) your combined income is more than $44,000, and 3) the tax rates move to around 50 percent (not implausible)? Your $5,000 could be cut to $2,875 ($5,000 minus half of 85 percent, or $4,250, equaling a potential-but-realistic tax hit of $2,125 out of your $5,000)!

Stopping the Bleeding

There are options that make sense for many retirees and pre-retirees who want to reduce their tax liability legally and legitimately.

One option is rolling your nest egg into an instrument known as a *Roth IRA*. This income tool is not ideal for everyone, but it has proven to be a smart move for many retirees.

Make no mistake: A Roth conversion does trigger a taxable event at the time of conversion, but the money grows from that point forward on a tax-free basis. All growth and withdrawals from then on would be tax-free. So for some nest eggs, it's a good move.

The *best* move is to have a retirement expert specializing in IRA distribution run the numbers for *your* nest egg to learn whether a Roth IRA might be a good option.

There might be even better options available to you, which move your money out of harm's way and give you that *guaranteed income for life.*

* * *

From sales tax to income tax, there are many obvious ways for the government to crack into your nest egg. Then there are the hidden taxes we've explored in some detail here.

But are there even *more* potential hidden cracks? Unfortunately, yes, there are. In the next chapter, we'll explore one of the biggest and most hard-to-plan-for types of "tax" headed your way.

Chapter 7

Inflation: Another Hidden Tax

There's an old funny story about how not-so-funny runaway inflation can be, and it goes something like this:

Back in the late twenties during the Weimar Republic in Germany, inflation had become so bad that the old German mark had become nearly worthless. A loaf of bread costs a million marks. One day, an old woman loaded a million marks into her wheelbarrow and rolled it into town. She left the money on the sidewalk outside the bakery and stepped inside to buy her bread. When she and the baker went outside to collect the cash, they discovered all the money neatly piled on the sidewalk. But the wheelbarrow (which had value) had been stolen.

I don't know if the story is true, and I doubt bread will ever cost a million bucks in this country. But we can be sure of one thing: Whatever items like bread, gasoline, and medicine cost today, they will likely cost more by the time you're, say, ten years into your retirement. The socioeconomic forces we've covered so far, from government funding of entitlement programs to fluctuations in the stock market, virtually assure us of significant inflation in the not-so-distant future.

How much inflation? No one knows for sure, of course. That's what makes inflation so difficult for retirees to plan for, which, in turn, amplifies the need for a *guaranteed income for life.*

"Printing" Money

I recently took cash from the ATMs (three machines in three days). And every twenty-dollar bill I received was perfectly crisp and new—as if it had just come off the press! I had to check to be sure the ink was dry. (It was.)

The experience brought to mind the fact that the government is printing *a lot* of money these days.

The government is indeed printing paper money at a rate much higher than the replacement rate of old and retired bills. But that's small potatoes compared to the amount of money the government "prints" electronically with activities known as *quantitative easing.*

The school of thought that calls for more government involvement in the economy (rather than less) prescribes quantitative easing as a way to try to help the overall economy by injecting more cash into the banking system. The theory is that the big banks will loan more money, which will then be put to work earning more revenue to be taxed.

It doesn't always work out as prescribed. (Critics often ask, "What government program does?") In some cases, the extra money gets bottled up and held by the banks rather than loaned. This is not mysterious: Quantitative easing measures are usually employed during times of weakness in the economy (which means fewer borrowers are willing to roll the dice on entrepreneurial ventures, and banks are highly likely to have tightened their credit requirements for those who are willing to borrow).

Wherever the extra "printed" money ends up, the dilution of the value of a dollar is the unavoidable chilling effect on the economy. When dollars are scarce, like anything, they're worth more. When there's a sea of them floating around out there, they're worth less.

This means the average consumer's *buying power* is reduced. As a result, more of those less-valuable dollars are required to pay bills and buy everyday necessities as prices rise to compensate for the increase—some say glut—in the monetary supply.

It doesn't mean you'll need a wheelbarrow of cash when you visit the grocery store (at least not in the near future). But it does mean you'll need a fatter wallet or, more appropriate to today's methodology, a bigger balance on your debit card.

Other Stealth Taxes

So your direct tax payments are headed upward, and the value of the money with which you'll have to pay those taxes (and everything else) is headed downward due to recent socioeconomic trends and developments.

I'm sorry to say so, but that's not all you have to worry about in terms of inflation and other unknowns that will likely have adverse effects on your nest egg. Here are some other stealth or hidden taxes which may be coming soon:

- *Value-Added Tax (VAT)*. For years, U.S. government officials have been offering proposals for the kind of VAT used by nations in the European Union. VAT plans essentially tax every phase of production and marketing needed to get a product into your hands. For example, as prescribed in some proposals, raw material producers add tax to the materials they sell manufacturers, manufacturers of parts add more tax before selling to assembly plants, assemblers add tax before selling to wholesalers, wholesalers collect tax from retailers, and (of course) the retailer adds tax to your receipt at checkout. The consumer's price goes up significantly to cover these many "bites" the government takes out of the entire economic process.

- *International trade policies.* When trade wars break out between nations or existing trade deals aren't negotiated fairly, there is a substantial impact on the prices paid for everything from widgets to medicine as countries add tariffs to the price of imported merchandise before selling it domestically.

- *Confusing legislative mandates.* The price of health care has already gone up significantly as a result of recent changes to federal health policy. The Affordable Care Act's impact can be extremely difficult to sort out and understand, especially for older folks who are the most affected by the changes. Even many financial experts have difficulty deciphering the code and making solid recommendations to their clients.

I'm reminded of a recent couple of younger female clients, each paying $600 per month for health care coverage. By finding better financial instruments to address what they needed, we reduced that monthly bill to $60. (They hugged me!)

The Bottom Line (Good and Bad)

Not to sound like a broken record, but we're all going to need more money in retirement than we thought (in most cases, *a lot* more). You're going to pay more for everything—from shoelaces to heart medication—than your dad or granddad had to pay.

That's the bad news.

The good news is that you have access to some great financial tools, no matter how big your nest egg, that Dad and Granddad didn't have. And these tools might just be the right answer for you as you puzzle through how to handle your retirement nest egg in the twenty-first century.

Perhaps the most powerful tool in your twenty-first century toolbox is one that has quite unfairly been given a bad name in recent years. But it's new and improved and is a fantastic fit for many retirees who appreciate the value of a *guaranteed income for life.*

Let's examine this potent tool next.

Chapter 8

The "A" Word: Annuities

When I say the word annuity to a new or prospective client, I sometimes get a negative reaction. "Annuities! Those are bad, aren't they? I heard a national finance expert say so on the radio just the other day!"

I'm not shocked by this reaction. Over the years, I've grown to expect it in some cases. That's because I know there's a lot of confusion out there, and many people have formed negative impressions of the "A" word based on incomplete or inaccurate information.

And a good percentage of those who start by saying they don't like annuities aren't really clear on what an annuity actually is.

An annuity is a financial or investment instrument that pays the beneficiary a defined *guaranteed* amount in periodic installments (generally monthly). Once these distribution payments begin, they usually last for the lifetime of the investor or beneficiary.

It turns out many people are more familiar with the annuity concept (and more amenable to it) than they realize. Your granddad's pension was a type of annuity. So is your Social Security benefit.

People sometimes say they don't like annuities—but I've never heard *anyone* tell me they didn't like that Social Security check arriving in their mailbox or bank account each month!

Once clients learn what an annuity truly is and what I mean when I say the "A" word, they relax. Retirees absolutely love the worry-free security a good annuity product can provide.

Not All Annuities Are Created Equal

I know a few nationally recognized and media-promoted expert financial advisors continually preach against annuities. And with regard to the type of annuity they recommend against, I'm generally in total agreement.

That's because the product they're warning against is almost always a *variable annuity,* which is a type of annuity that's tied to the stock market and all its volatility. It's the last thing you want for the money you're counting on to last the rest of your life.

Since variable annuities are tied to the stock market, they look great when the market is booming. But, as we covered earlier, the market doesn't always boom. It suffers corrections all the time. And when that happens, an investor whose money is tied up in a variable annuity could end up losing a substantial portion of the savings they've worked so hard to accumulate.

Granddad's pension was not a variable annuity. It was guaranteed income he could count on, month in and month out, for the rest of his life. In the case of many pension plans, when Granddad passed away, the checks went to Grandma for the rest of *her* life.

CHAPTER 8: THE "A" WORD

Variable annuities can provide a kind of *guaranteed income for life.* However, considering the extra fees they carry compared to fixed annuities, those national experts might have a point when they warn that a variable annuity leaves you with guaranteed *worry* for life!

A few years ago, there were so many highly promoted and aggressively marketed variable annuity products out there that the "A" word gained (and deserved) a pretty bad reputation. Too many retirees were harmed (even wiped out) because they put too much of their trust and their nest egg into these iffy products.

Times Have Changed, and So Have Annuities

The only way to get that all-important *guaranteed income for life* is to move at least a significant chunk of your nest egg into a *fixed* annuity. Fixed annuities have been around for more than a century, and no one has ever lost a penny investing in a fixed annuity.

Fixed annuities were always there—right alongside those variable annuity products—but during the heyday of variable annuity marketing, the fixed annuity didn't look so attractive. Variable annuity sellers could show impressive growth numbers, and they liked to show prospects those numbers alongside the low-growth fixed annuities, which were earning what salespeople called *bank interest.*

You can see what an easy sell that was for so many retirement- and pre-retirement-aged folks.

For people who haven't saved as much as they would have liked for their retirement, bank interest doesn't look like it will get them the growth they need to have enough money in retirement. That's why people jumped at the chance to invest in variable annuities or leave their nest eggs otherwise entangled with the stock market.

The answer was to create annuity products that could offer modest growth during strong periods of overall economic performance but not lose money during stock market downturns.

The *fixed index annuity* product was born!

These annuities offer exactly what retirees want most: modest growth, no chance of losses, and a worry-free *guaranteed income for life.*

But unfortunately, since the "A" word is attached to these products—and since so much attention has now been paid to criticizing *variable* annuity products—too many people hear the word annuity and run in the opposite direction.

Many aren't even aware of these fantastic new investment tools that can offer a true worry-free retirement.

It's Important to Do Your Research

Annuities are NOT bad, despite what you might have heard on the radio or elsewhere. But you have to do your research or get advice from a true professional who specializes in these kinds of products to make sure you're getting the right annuity product.

Annuities are not one-size-fits-all, and like stock market investing, they're not the only answer for every retiree. But in most cases, having at least a substantial portion of your nest egg moved out of harm's way and into a FIA is a smart choice.

Things seem to have changed at the speed of light over the last few months and years. We've all had to adjust our thinking on just about everything, from how close to stand to one another to what medicines to take. In the past, if you heard something on the radio or television, it was pretty much "gospel." Now, that's far from the case.

It's important for retirees to take another look at things they may not have fully understood, given the rapid changes in the financial markets. Annuities are at the top of that list.

Consider the Source

When you're talking to a financial advisor or watching a commercial on television, and it becomes apparent that you're being steered toward high-growth, market-based investments, it's a good idea to assess the motivations behind what you're hearing.

A financial advisor who specializes in *accumulation* will focus on those market-based solutions because the high potential upside is the centerpiece of their practice. They're not focused on *distribution*—maybe that's something they figure you can worry about later—and therefore, they aren't primarily motivated to find you *guaranteed income for life*.

Meanwhile, a large brokerage firm that runs ads proclaiming we'll all need "a million dollars" in retirement might be motivated by the large asset management fees that are their bread and butter.

(As a side note, one large brokerage firm, J.P. Morgan, recently published an insight piece that signaled a shift in the firm's views, putting more emphasis on annuities for retiring clients and less emphasis on riskier market-based products.)

In recent years, no less a luminary than the *Wall Street Journal* has published findings that indicate owners of annuities—retirees who've established for themselves a *guaranteed income for life*—are happier in retirement and tend to *live longer.*

That is what many of my clients enjoy, which is why I suggest a reset in thinking for prospective clients who have been advised to focus on accumulation in the past and may not have given much thought to how their nest eggs can pay them an income for the rest of their lives.

You don't have to fear the "A" word!

Break Away from Fear

Those TV "experts" who say we all need a million dollars in a brokerage account by age sixty-five are not necessarily focused on what's best for retirement-aged clients.

They're more likely focused on what's best for their brokerage firms, and they're playing on your fear in order to keep you from moving your money into an asset that can provide you with that peace of mind and away from the accounts that provide them with high management fees.

I don't know many people who have a million dollars in a brokerage account. But I do know many who have been made to feel unworthy because they don't have that account. As a result, they're paralyzed by fear, scared to spend any money, and afraid to move it away from their "trusted" stockbrokers.

Meanwhile, these folks are NOT enjoying their retirement. Instead, they're worried (and not as likely to live the long and happy life indicated by those *Wall Street Journal* findings). And their money stays in those brokerage accounts, gaining and losing value as the market continues its shifts, generating hefty fees for the brokers.

Chapter 8: The "A" Word

A retirement advisor who focuses on *distribution* can help you break away from that paralyzing fear. I do this for my clients all the time. I tell clients that if they create a pension for themselves, they can spend more of their time enjoying retirement and less worrying about how much money they have in the bank.

You're not unworthy if you don't have a million dollars. I promise you that you can achieve an enjoyable retirement and peace of mind with a lot less than a million dollars.

Retirees who have come to understand the comfort that comes with their *guaranteed income for life* have Social Security and fixed-annuity payouts (very much like Granddad's old pension) that arrive in their bank accounts every month, month in and month out. With that comes peace of mind and the ability to enjoy the retirement they have worked so hard to earn.

These folks broke away from the fear that would have kept their nest eggs at the mercy of a volatile stock market. They've discovered (or rediscovered) the reasons fixed index annuities have become so popular among retirees.

And they've broken away from an accumulation-based mindset that would not serve them well in their retirement years.

I can personally attest to the peaceful feeling you get when you know you'll have money coming in regularly once the regular paychecks stop coming in.

I practice what I preach. I'm fifty-four years of age, and I'm planning on working many more years. And since I'm not yet retired, I do have some money in online brokerage accounts.

But my weapon of choice for my retirement years? You guessed it: the *fixed annuity.*

I don't have a fixed annuity; I have three of them (so far)! And after having to listen to me extol the virtues of a *guaranteed income for life* and hearing about how fixed annuities give my clients such peace of mind, my wife decided she would get an annuity too.

We have other accounts, just like many of my clients do, but it's the money we're investing in these annuity accounts that will provide us with the same guaranteed retirement my clients (and millions of others across the country) enjoy.

* * *

As you approach retirement, try to find an advisor who specializes in these particular tailor-made retirement products, one who you can get to know, like, and trust. Getting your nest egg into the right position to provide you with a *guaranteed income for life* is one of the greatest gifts you and your spouse can give yourselves.

Speaking of gifts, the next chapter talks about one of the greatest gifts you can give the *rest* of your family—especially your adult children.

Let's look at planning for your long-term care.

Chapter 9

Long-Term Care: A Gift for Your Family

A s we age into retirement and our golden years begin to unfold, things we only dreamed of doing during our working years suddenly become realistic possibilities.

Retired people who have established a *guaranteed income for life* spend less time worrying about finances and can devote time to beloved hobbies, such as gardening, cooking, golfing, fishing, finishing projects in the garage (and elsewhere), reading, photography, and other creative and recreational endeavors.

Many retirees dream of travel, and many find that they can make it a reality during their newfound time off. For many people, the opportunity to travel and see the world (and the grandkids) is one of the main things they've been looking forward to in retirement. And now, with their careers finished and finances arranged, many can take advantage of travel opportunities.

Of course, none of us can live forever, and as we age, we experience the health impacts and ability changes that age brings. Retirees who have waited their whole lives to travel and take on new activities find that they progress through three phases of retirement.

- **The Go-Go Phase.** During this phase, a retiree's health and vitality permit them to do just about anything they want to do.
- **The Slow-Go Phase.** This phase is marked by declining vitality. Many (even most) of their favorite activities are still possible, but they have to take it a little easier.
- **The No-Go Phase.** A senior enters this phase when it's just too tough to get up and down in the garden or handle the rigors of travel. Life can still be quite enjoyable, but declining health and vitality curtail a retiree's activity (and mobility). They can enjoy themselves in many ways, but they largely have to stay put.

This progression is different for everyone. Retired couples often find that one spouse progresses more quickly to the next phase than does the other. So it's not uncommon to see someone who could travel and do more simply decline to be as active because they choose to take care of their spouse and do things at a slower pace to spend time with them.

Eventually, all retirees end up in the latter stages of the No-Go phase, and they need to be cared for; there are simply some basic things they can no longer do for themselves.

That's when LTC comes into play. Whether through the government (via Medicaid), adult children, or professionals paid by the retiree's LTC insurance, someone has to help older folks enjoy the best quality of life possible at the very end of their long lives.

Activities of Daily Living

Experts have identified several Activities of Daily Living (ADLs) that determine a person's general level of ability to function on a daily basis. Different organizations and experts have come up with different lists of ADLs, but these six are generally agreed upon by a rough consensus:

- *Eating.* Some seniors have difficulty feeding themselves for a variety of reasons.
- *Bathing.* This includes getting in and out of the shower or tub and performing basic grooming functions, such as shaving and brushing one's teeth.
- *Dressing.* Is the senior able to dress and undress without struggling too much with things like buttons and zippers?
- *Transferring.* This is a familiar activity for elderly folks—being able to stand and change locations, such as from a chair to a bed or from bed to a wheelchair.
- *Toileting.* Is the senior able to get on and off the toilet without assistance?
- *Continence.* This ADL refers to a senior's ability to control bladder and bowel functions.

LTC through Medicare doesn't kick in until a senior can't do two or more of these ADLs without help. Insurers that provide LTC coverage have different lists and functionality thresholds that trigger LTC benefits.

It's worth noting that Medicare doesn't pay much toward LTC (short-term rehabilitation only). So once Medicare kicks in, it continues covering skilled care only when a patient is improving (and is expected to return home from the skilled-care facility after rehabilitation).

Medicaid, by contrast, pays for LTC once the patient has exhausted their savings—obviously not a desirable situation for this and many other reasons.

As I mentioned, there are other lists of daily activities that many experts (and seniors) consider important, though not as critical as the six ADLs. These activities, known as Instrumental Activities of Daily Living (IADLs), might include keeping a home safe, using a telephone, managing medications, housekeeping, shopping, and caring for pets. These are tricky activities for many seniors, but they aren't necessarily required for everyone or for every day.

However, whether it's Medicare, Medicaid, insurance—or care from family members—a senior needs help with daily living when they can no longer do some combination of these activities on their own.

Family Caregivers

One very common scenario happens when family members care for seniors who don't have good LTC coverage. Usually, this means their adult children are the ones burdened with helping their folks get through each day.

This scenario can progress through phases too. For example, at first, an adult son or daughter who lives nearby might just drop in and check on their parents on a weekly or semiweekly basis. Later, those check-ins might need to happen once or twice a day. In many cases, adult children eventually have to rearrange their lives and live with their parents to ensure they're as safe, comfortable, and happy as possible.

Chapter 9: Long-Term Care

If you've had experience as a family caregiver, you know what those who haven't don't know: It often requires so much of you that you have to put your own life on hold to take loving care of your parents in the latter stages of their No-Go years.

By the way, this doesn't usually happen when you have the energy of a thirty- or thirty-five-year-old. So, by the time your folks need this type of daily care, you usually have to do this significant work when you're in your fifties or sixties.

Technically, you might be a senior yourself!

I have a friend who found himself caring for his wife's elderly parents. They were in the No-Go phase of retirement and needed daily help with cooking and other chores but were still living in the house they'd owned for more than forty years. Everyone knew it was nearing the time when they wouldn't be able to live on their own, but no one in the family was quite sure what was next. One thing the elderly parents were sure of, though: "We are NOT going to a nursing home! We refuse! Our kids promised us long ago never to stick us in one of those places!"

Now, some retirement homes are quite nice. But these seniors didn't have that frame of reference, and they were quite adamant about staying at home to the very end.

One morning, while my friend was washing the dishes after serving his in-laws breakfast, they started going on about how they would never (ever) go to a nursing home.

My friend, possessed with a sense of humor, finally replied, "I know, Mom and Dad, but I think my wife and I might look into it. We're old enough, and some of these places are pretty nice. That way, maybe somebody could take care of us so that we'd still have the energy to keep taking care of you!"

Everyone laughed, but the point was made. Eldercare can really take it out of you.

Imagine this: You're at or near retirement age your-self—your Go-Go years—and you're maintaining not one household but two (including your parents' place). You feel like you need to be on call around the clock, and you can't travel unless you can find someone to cover for you in terms of caring for the folks. And every day, your parents seem to need more and more help.

Elderly parents are often aware of the impact caring for them has on their adult children. They see how their kids' lives have been put on hold to take care of them, just at the time when those kids should be traveling and seeing the world (the way they did during their own Go-Go years in many cases). Some confront this guilt by claiming they don't need as much help as they do. Others just keep apolo-gizing and feeling trapped in an elderly lifestyle they never wanted or anticipated.

That's why securing LTC coverage *before* you need it is such a wonderful gift to give your entire family.

The peace of mind you feel when you have a *guaran-teed income for life* is multiplied when you know your family won't be burdened with your care when you can no longer do everything for yourself.

Timing Is Everything

Nobody likes to think about getting old and frail at a time when they're still relatively young and robust. Intellectually, we all know that we probably have it coming, but many people who are approaching retirement haven't considered the LTC they're likely to need later in life. It's almost as if they don't really believe it can happen to them.

Here's the rub: You can get the best LTC coverage at the best rates and with the greatest benefits if you arrange for the coverage when you're young and healthy.

People who are approaching retirement age and have had the experience of caring for elderly family members tend to understand this more clearly; many people in this situation seek out LTC coverage at a time when they can still get a good plan.

If you wait until you're in your late seventies or eighties when the need arises, you'll find it very difficult—quite likely, impossible—to get good LTC coverage.

LTC insurers require their clients to pass physicals. Unfortunately, by the time you are struggling with the ADLs and IADLs we've described, you're a lot less likely to be able to do that.

When that's the case, your options are limited. Some degree of LTC from the government is available in the form of Medicare (very limited, I might add), or you might be able to take advantage of veteran benefits if you served in the military.

But many folks in this situation end up relying on their adult offspring to put their own lives on hold to take care of them. The opportunity to give them the amazing gift of LTC coverage and to remove that burden from their shoulders has passed.

Long-Term Care Is More Important than Ever

The need for LTC coverage points out another reason we're all likely to need more money in retirement than we may have thought we'd need.

As mentioned previously, we're living longer. In the days of Granddad's pension, folks retired at sixty-five, but they didn't tend to live long past their sixties. So their Go-Go, Slow-Go, and No-Go phases might well have come in months, not years, with one following fast on the heels of the other.

Chronic illnesses and cognitive problems weren't things too many of our grandparents had to deal with. But as life expectancies increase, this latest generation of retirement-aged folks suffer a variety of age-related maladies. Some had comfortable and sedentary desk jobs for many years and didn't experience the kind of hard work their grandparents had to do (which kept them more physically fit). So it's a trade-off: We live longer these days, but we're likely to suffer all kinds of health problems previous generations didn't face.

And how do we pay for the health care we need to address these problems? Again, inflation and higher taxes combine to drive our health care costs higher and higher while reducing the discretionary income we have available to pay those skyrocketing costs.

For many, the solution is a strong program of LTC coverage that will take care of what they really will need as the sun sets on their lives.

Many Great LTC Products to Choose From

The standard LTC policy—available to those who can afford the premiums and pass the required physical exams—includes benefits triggered when the insured loses the ability to perform some combination of ADLs.

Those benefits will range from periodic home visits by health and assisted-living professionals to a residence in facilities where the beneficiary can get constant supervised care if they need it.

Our faithful friend, the *fixed annuity*, can also come into play when you find an annuity with an *LTC rider*. Your money can experience modest growth and be available either to you as guaranteed income or to your caregivers in the event you need LTC.

Some LTC programs include a death benefit, which can be paid to your spouse or another beneficiary if you pass away before your LTC benefits run out.

There's a wide variety of LTC products on the market today, providing an almost endless array of choices in combining LTC, annuities, and life insurance. It's best to check with your retirement advisor, one who understands the details of LTC as well as income distribution, to find the right plan for you and/or your spouse.

Don't Grow Old Without a Plan

LTC is simply one thing many retirement-aged folks haven't thought about. And too many don't think about it until it's too late to get good coverage.

Some people assume the government will take care of their LTC needs when the time comes. But if you're trusting your care to the government, are you likely to get the best care?

Medicaid can help Americans who have no other recourse, but it can't provide everything a good LTC policy can give you.

In Sweden, the government does provide LTC. But to pay for it, local taxes are in the neighborhood of 70 percent. And it's still government health care.

Those who have a *true plan* for their retirement, with *true guarantees* for income and LTC, tend to have the happiest and longest retirements. More Go-Go years—thanks to reduced stress and worry— and more help when the No-Go years arrive.

Chapter 10

The Holy Grail:
Guaranteed Income for Life

If you think about it, very few things in life are guaranteed. They say there are only two sure things —death and taxes—and I suppose that's true. And we're reasonably certain the sun will rise in the east and set in the west tomorrow.

But when it comes to retirement, what can you really count on? Can anyone guarantee that the money you've invested in the stock market will continue to grow and always be there for you? No. Can anyone guarantee that the nice interest rate you might be getting on a certain investment, like a CD, will always be available? No.

That's why a large and growing number of retirement-aged folks are taking a fresh look at *fixed index annuities* and the possibility of establishing for themselves a *guaranteed income for life*.

And it's why the focus of my practice is on helping those folks and why I love doing what I do.

Nothing Variable About It

As I mentioned earlier, a lot of folks have developed a negative impression of annuities. They've only heard about one type of annuity—the *variable* annuity, which is still anchored in the stock market, and they've heard horror stories about people who've lost much of their nest egg by relying on these risky investments.

Variable annuities looked great at one time, because some sellers were able to show huge growth numbers. But again, just as the stock market tends to show overall gains over time, it also experiences major "corrections" at times. At those times, you can lose much of your savings if you're invested in variable annuities.

There's nothing guaranteed about that! And that's why I don't work with variable annuities. I work with fixed index annuities because they provide *guaranteed income for life*—and there's nothing variable about that!

My advice to retirement-aged folks who are exploring their options and have developed a negative notion about annuities is to take another look. Do some research, and you'll discover that not all annuities are the same. And while variable annuities are risky, fixed index annuities are not. With these fantastic financial income tools, you can make sure your nest egg continues to grow at a reasonable rate and that it will always be there for you, offering you the kind of peace of mind you can only get with a *guaranteed income for life*.

Peace of Mind for Anyone

Just about anyone who's disciplined and committed to their planning can take advantage of these excellent tools to give themselves a *guaranteed income for life*.

You'll likely see many ads from financial advisors who want to work with you—but only if you have $500,000 or more in your portfolio. I don't know too many people in that situation, which is why I like to work with the unserved or underserved part of the market, comprised of people who have a smaller nest egg they really need to protect. In my view, the less money you have, the more important it is to protect it, getting it out of the stock market and out of harm's way.

It's just a matter of understanding three things. First, you need to understand that we're all going to need more money in retirement than we may originally have thought we would need. Second, it's important to be realistic about the unknowns I've described in previous chapters. And third, you need to reassess what may be long-held beliefs about what kinds of investments work for retirees and which offer far more risk than they're worth.

In other words, it's a matter of understanding the real need for that *guaranteed income for life.*

Here's to a Longer, Happier Life

To review, here are the things that keep a lot of retirement-aged folks up at night:

- *Inflation.* Yes, just when you have less money to spend, your dollars will not stretch as far as they used to. Everything costs more than it did the previous year, from gasoline to milk to medicine.
- *Taxes.* As the value of the dollar goes down, the number of dollars the government takes increases. Why? The country and the states are growing, and more citizens need and demand more government services. Who pays for those services? You do.

- *Women's special needs.* As I've detailed, women have specific and different needs in retirement planning for a variety of reasons than do men (particularly their husbands). These concerns keep women up at night—but they also trouble the men who care about those women.

- *No more pensions.* While our granddads simply didn't have to worry about their monthly pension checks, today's retirees have a lot more to think about in the age of 401(k) plans, IRAs, and other often-volatile instruments that make managing one's retirement nest egg a real DIY project these days.

- *Less general stability.* We live in ever-changing times, politically and financially—much more so than the more predictable environment in which previous generations entered retirement. Will political changes affect the stock market? Will upheaval rock the economy even more than in recent years? Will we see more global pandemics? Lots of questions to keep seniors up at night, and there are very few reliable answers.

- *Longer lives.* It's obvious that you'll need more money in retirement if you're going to enjoy a longer retirement! And with lifespans much greater than they were a few years ago (and continuing to grow), people worry more and more about outliving their savings or, in many cases, dying before they can put a solid plan in place.

- *Health and wellness.* The last chapter discussed this in great detail. We live longer, but the quality of our lives is not the same at the end of a long retirement as it is at the beginning, simply because the human body does not last forever. Planning for LTC (or even basic health care) during retirement is a major worry for many folks and their families.

Add up all these worries, and you get the one thing seniors definitely don't need: stress. The result of stress is shorter, sadder lives.

I love the result of my work because it reduces a great deal of that stress and gives my clients the chance to live longer, happier lives. And it's all because they're able to establish a true *guaranteed income for life* for themselves.

Take a fresh look at what you can achieve with fixed index annuities. (I've heard my clients refer to these instruments as "sleep insurance" because it allows them to sleep well at night.)

Conclusion

A New ERA:
Skipping the Worry of Retirement

I was blessed to have been a fairly talented pitcher on my high school baseball team, and I landed a full scholarship to play baseball at North Carolina State University. I had a nice college career at NC State, and I think I'm still in the school's record books in fifth or sixth place for all-time wins.

Pitchers (and baseball enthusiasts in general) tend to keep track of several types of statistics that help them monitor individual and team performance. The number of wins a pitcher can record is a major example of those individual-player stats.

As a pitcher, you also keep track of your strikeouts, how many batters you walk, and really, just about everything that can be measured and recorded. But the big one is your earned run average—your ERA.

The ERA is a statistic that calculates the average number of runs a pitcher gives up over the course of nine innings (the regulation length of a game). Each game has nine innings, and each inning affords your opponent the chance to keep sending batters up to face you until you get three of them out. So if you were to pitch a complete game (which doesn't often happen in reality) and record those twenty-seven outs, your ERA would be calculated by the number of runs you gave up in the course of getting those outs.

Famous pitchers like Nolan Ryan and Roger Clemens have extremely low lifetime ERA statistics, compiled throughout their successful careers (which, of course, is what makes them famous). Anything around 2.0 earned runs per nine innings is a phenomenal stat for a pitcher.

As I mentioned, I did have a pretty successful baseball career at NC State. But you wouldn't have known it from the way things went in the first game of my sophomore season. I managed to record one out in the first inning in that game, but our opponents had already scored three runs. So the coach took me out of the game—I just didn't have the right stuff that day.

Three earned runs, one-third of an inning. The baseball enthusiasts and math whizzes among you will be quick to note that my ERA for that season, at that point, was 81. Not very Ryan- or Clemens-like!

It was bad that I had to endure my teammates' teasing about having such a horrible, published ERA to start the season. But the worst part was that I had to wait a whole week before I could get back out there and work to lower that number! I did—over the course of the season—but I had sure dug myself a deep hole to climb out of (statistically speaking).

Why do I tell this embarrassing story? Because it stuck with me, it motivated me, and I never forgot the power of the ERA.

Many years later, in my business career, I developed a different type of ERA system to help my clients gain clarity in their retirement planning.

Here's the ERA plan I encourage my clients to observe: *E* stands for **evaluate**. Before you can achieve any goal, you have to evaluate your current situation. If you want to lose twenty pounds, for instance, you need to evaluate what you currently weigh (as well as what you're doing in terms of diet and exercise) to truly understand your current circumstances. Retirement planning is no different. So one of the first things I do for my clients is a full evaluation of their current financial circumstances.

R stands for **results**. Once you have a firm grasp of your current situation, you need to determine which results are important to you. Is it protecting yourself from running out of money? Traveling or making improvements to your home? Leaving money to your family? Reducing what you pay in taxes and fees? All of these things are good, but they're not equally important to everyone. The results each client wants will differ.

Finally, the *A* in my system stands for **actions**. Once we've done our evaluation and determined our desired results, I always present an action plan to my clients—steps they can take now to achieve those results down the road.

This last part is critical. I'll admit there have been times in my life when I've studied facts and weighed pros and cons—and then failed to take any action. And when you don't take action, nothing happens! You make no progress toward your goals.

The same goes for my clients. Of course, they differ in terms of evaluating their current circumstances and determining their desired results, but every client needs to take actions to move toward those results.

I always tell my clients that they don't have to implement everything in the plan all at once. Many clients start with a handful of the proposed actions, and they often add more a few years later as they begin to see their results.

End Your ERA of Worry

If you're tired of lying awake at night, worrying about everything from inflation to taxes to health care, reach out to my office, and let me "pitch" you something different.

See if you can catch on to the "sleep insurance" you can get from a *guaranteed income for life*.

My clients tend to sleep pretty well. They worry less. They live longer, happier lives than they would have lived with the stress of dealing with a risky retirement.

I'd love to help you become the next retiree to get that kind of peace of mind.

You can reach me by phone at (336) 746-4729 or by email at brad@bradrhodesfinancial.com. And you can learn more by visiting either of these websites:
— BradRhodesFinancial.com
— BradRhodes.RetireVillage.com

About the Author

Brad Rhodes is the founder and president of BradRhodesFinancial.com. He specializes in helping retirees and pre-retirees avoid the financial pitfalls that threaten their happy retirements. Brad loves his work and his clients, both face-to-face and as host of *Safe Money Radio*. He truly enjoys presenting opportunities and strategies that help individuals and couples retire with a *guaranteed income for life*.

Since 1992, Brad has had the very good fortune of being trained by one of the best financial educators in the country—his dad. And from his dad, he learned early on that you need two things to succeed in a career of financial advice. First, you need to concentrate on the needs of others before yourself; second, it's important to treat folks the way you would want people to treat your mom.

Brad lives in Lexington, North Carolina, with his wife, Jackie. He is the proud father of two daughters, Tori and Ashley.

"With the uncertainty in today's economic environment, I can sleep at night knowing that my clients have never lost a dime of their retirement funds when they've followed our recommendations. There is something special about helping people enjoy true peace of mind about their retirement future. It is my sincere wish to give you that peace of mind."

—*Brad Rhodes*

Expert
Press

www.ExpertPress.net

Made in United States
North Haven, CT
23 December 2021

13564585R00055